GARLIC

GARLIC

INTRODUCTION BY SUE LAWRENCE

southwater

This edition is published by Southwater

Southwater is an imprint of
Anness Publishing Limited
Hermes House
88–89 Blackfriars Road
London SE1 8HA
tel. 020 7401 2077
fax 020 7633 9499

Distributed in the UK by
The Manning Partnership
251–253 London Road East
Batheaston
Bath BA1 7RL
tel. 01225 852 727
fax 01225 852 852

Distributed in the USA by
Anness Publishing Inc.
27 West 20th Street
Suite 504
New York
NY 10011
tel. 212 807 6739
fax 212 807 6813

Distributed in Australia by
Sandstone Publishing
Unit 1
360 Norton Street
Leichhardt
New South Wales 2040
tel. 02 9560 7888
fax 02 9560 7488

© 1996, 2000 Anness Publishing Limited

1 3 5 7 9 10 8 6 4 2

Publisher Joanna Lorenz
Senior Cookery Editor Linda Fraser
Cookery Editor Anne Hildyard
Designer Lisa Tai
Illustrations Anna Koska
Photographers Karl Adamson, Edward Allwright, Steve Baxter,
James Duncan and Amanda Heywood
Recipes Annie Nichols and Nicola Diggins
Food for photography Elizabeth Wolf-Cohen, Wendy Lee,
Jenny Shapter and Jane Stevenson
Stylists Madeleine Brehaut, Hilary Guy, Blake Minton and Kirsty Rawlings

For all recipes, quantities are given in both metric and imperial measures and, where appropriate, measures are also given in standard cups and spoons. Follow one set, but not a mixture, because they are not interchangeable.

Previously published as *Cooking with Garlic*

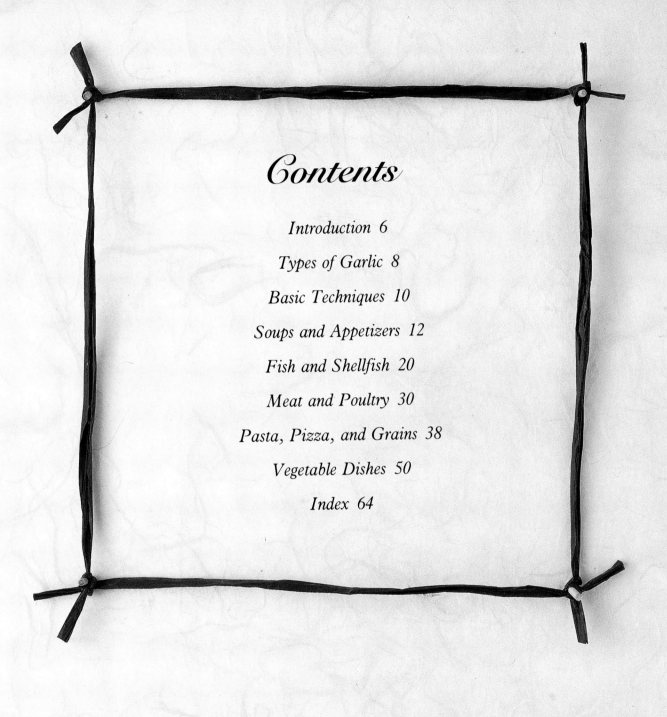

Contents

Introduction 6

Types of Garlic 8

Basic Techniques 10

Soups and Appetizers 12

Fish and Shellfish 20

Meat and Poultry 30

Pasta, Pizza, and Grains 38

Vegetable Dishes 50

Index 64

$\mathscr{I}$NTRODUCTION

$\mathbf{H}$ow did we manage without it? No, not plastic wrap or microwave, but garlic. All those years the French were drowning their snails in garlic butter and the Italians were flooding their spaghetti in garlic and olive oil, we were high and dry. A desert. Only over the past 30 years or so has garlic become not only an acceptable ingredient, but an essential one.

Some of the most popular dishes using garlic are garlic bread and roast garlic lamb. Garlic bread is still a classic .at all sorts of parties where fresh garlic is mixed with butter and salt to make a delicious butter to fill the loaf. Then there is roast lamb, spiked with slivers of fresh garlic and often sprigs of rosemary: the resulting aroma is truly irresistible. Add a dish of sautéed potatoes, a glass of hearty red wine and you could be in heaven. (Or at least in sunny Provence.)

Most of my early garlic memories come from France. I well remember chicken baked with three bulbs of garlic; soup thickened with semolina and flavored only with bay and garlic. These were strong, punchy flavors – for garlic has, indeed, a pungent taste. But once you know a few tricks about this versatile bulb, antisocial aromas become of little consequence. For example, as a general rule, the more finely garlic is chopped – or crushed – the more

potent it will be. Raw garlic is far more pungent than cooked. If you want to add simply a background flavor, drop a whole unpeeled clove into a stock, sauce or casserole. Or roast or grill them whole, peeled or unpeeled. Then you can snip off the top of the unpeeled clove and squeeze out the sweet yet smoky-tasting contents into your mashed potato or salad dressing.

In this book, there are some lovely new ideas for its use. Garlic is more often associated with meat than fish, but there are some very interesting fish dishes in these pages: Hake in Wine and Garlic Sauce, Halibut with Garlic and Tomato Sauce, and Broiled Garlic Mussels. There are also fabulous vegetable dishes such as Eggplant and Roast Garlic Pâté, Garlicky Baked Squash, and Onion and Garlic Galettes. The garlic is used in variable quantities in all these dishes – either as a full, powerful flavor, or as a subtle, background taste which enhances all sorts of savory dishes.

There is one type of recipe which I am relieved to see omitted from this book: dessert dishes such as garlic ice-cream or sorbets. Like its fellow family members, the onion and chive, let us keep garlic – with all its glorious flavor – to savory dishes. This is where it has been used since ancient times; this is where it stars.

Sue Lawrence

TYPES OF GARLIC

WHITE GARLIC

This variety of garlic has a papery, silky skin. A single bulb consists of 8 to 10 plump cloves.

PURPLE GARLIC

Considered by many to have a superior flavor. The skin may be pink, violet, or purple.

ELEPHANT GARLIC

A large variety which is the mildest of all and can be cooked as a vegetable.

SMOKED GARLIC

Garlic can be smoked over a barbecue. It adds a delicate smoked flavor to fish and chicken dishes.

PICKLED GARLIC

Available in delicatessens and some specialty shops and comes in jars of either whole bulbs or separate cloves. It is very pungent, and easy to make at home.

GARLIC PEPPER AND SALT

These products, as their name implies, combine garlic with seasoning. Use in dressings, casseroles, or salads.

GARLIC PUREE

Convenient if fresh garlic is not at hand, but the flavor is not comparable.

DRIED GARLIC

Available minced, chopped, powdered, and in granules. In its dehydrated form, it is almost odorless, but when rehydrated the flavor is good. These forms of garlic are useful for adding to sauces, curries, soups, stews, salads, chutneys and pickles.

GARLIC BREAD SEASONING

A useful seasoning to make quick garlic butter which can be spread on French bread before baking. Also available is a seasoned garlic spread for the health conscious, made without butter.

White garlic

Garlic bread seasoning

Garlic purée

Garlic salt

Smoked garlic

Garlic pickle

Minced garlic

Pickled garlic

Garlic powder

Elephant garlic

Garlic cloves

Garlic purée

Garlic pepper

Dried chopped garlic

Garlic granules

Purple garlic

Pickled whole garlic

$\mathcal{B}$ASIC $\mathcal{T}$ECHNIQUES

PEELING AND CHOPPING GARLIC

Garlic is usually peeled of its papery skin before use, which can be a fussy operation if the garlic is very fresh. First, separate the cloves from the main bulb or pull single cloves from the bulb.

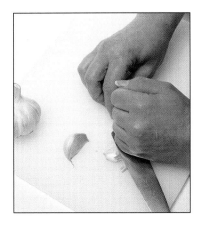

To peel, lay the flat side of a large knife on top of the garlic and bang gently to loosen the skin. Crush the peeled clove with the side of the knife to flatten it. Chop the garlic finely by holding the tip of the knife on the board and lifting only the handle end, moving the blade across the garlic. Garlic can also be crushed in a garlic crusher but this tends to give it a harsher flavor.

GARLIC BUTTER

Garlic butter can be prepared ahead and either chilled or frozen until required. To freeze, wrap well in plastic wrap and then in foil. The butter can be used straight from the freezer.

Place 4 ounces unsalted butter in a mixing bowl and beat with a wooden spoon or electric mixer until soft. Add 1–2 chopped garlic cloves and season to taste with pepper and salt. Blend together well.

Place the blended butter on a large piece of wax paper and shape it into a roll. Keep the butter and your hands cool while you do this. Wrap up the roll in the wax paper and chill until firm. Unwrap it and cut into discs.

GARLIC OIL

This oil takes on the delicious flavor of fresh garlic and is invaluable for enlivening salad dressings and sauces and for sautéeing. If the oil solidifies in the fridge, leave to soften at room temperature.

Trim the root ends from 6–8 cloves of fresh garlic. Bang them with the flat side of a knife to loosen the skin. Peel them with your fingers.

Hold the garlic cloves one at a time between thumb and finger and, using the flat side of a heavy knife near the handle, crush the cloves by pressing down heavily onto a chopping board.

Place all the crushed garlic in a screw-topped jar. Add ½ cup olive oil and cap. Store the oil for up to two weeks in a fridge.

Aioli   Serves 6–8

This rich garlicky mayonnaise is usually served with crudités as an hors d'oeuvre.

Put 4 crushed garlic cloves in a small bowl with a pinch of salt and blend together with the back of a spoon. Add 2 egg yolks and beat with an electric mixer for 30 seconds until slightly thickened and creamy. Beat in 1 cup olive oil: add it drop by drop until the mixture thickens, then add the olive oil in a thin stream. Thin the mayonnaise with a few drops of lemon juice and season to taste. Chill in the fridge for up to 2 days, then serve at room temperature.

Soups and Appetizers

Garlic adds unmistakable character to chilled

tomato soup and hearty fish or onion soups; imparts

taste-tingling flavor to dips; spikes up guacamole

and jazzes up simple salads.

CHILLED TOMATO AND GARLIC SOUP

This uncooked, garlicky soup can be made in minutes with the minimum of effort.

Serves 4–6

3–3½ pounds ripe tomatoes, peeled
   and roughly chopped

4 garlic cloves, crushed

2 tablespoons extra virgin olive
   oil (optional)

2 tablespoons balsamic vinegar

ground black pepper

4 slices whole wheat bread

low-fat ricotta cheese, to garnish

COOK'S TIP

*For the best flavor, it is
important to use only fully
ripened, succulent tomatoes
to make this soup.*

Place the tomatoes in a food processor or blender with the garlic and olive oil, if using. Blend until smooth.

Pass the mixture through a strainer to remove the seeds. Stir in the balsamic vinegar and season with pepper. Leave in the fridge to chill.

Toast the bread lightly. While still hot, cut off the crusts and slice in half horizontally. Place on a board with the uncooked sides facing down and, using a circular motion, rub to remove any doughy pieces of bread.

Cut each slice into four triangles. Place on a griddle and toast the uncooked sides until lightly golden. Garnish each bowl of soup with a spoonful of ricotta cheese and serve with the Melba toast.

ONION AND GARLIC SOUP

In France, this standard bistro fare is served so frequently, it is simply referred to as gratinée.

Serves 6–8

1 tablespoon butter

2 tablespoons olive oil

4 large onions, about 1½ pounds,
   thinly sliced

2–4 garlic cloves, finely chopped

1 teaspoon sugar

½ teaspoon dried thyme

2 tablespoons flour

½ cup dry white wine

8 cups chicken or beef broth

2 tablespoons brandy (optional)

6–8 thick slices French bread, toasted

1 garlic clove, halved

3 cups shredded Swiss cheese

Melt the butter together with the olive oil in a large, heavy-based saucepan or flameproof casserole. Add the onions and cook over moderately high heat for 10–12 minutes until softened and just beginning to brown. Add the finely chopped garlic, sugar, and dried thyme and continue cooking over moderate heat for 30–35 minutes until the onions are well browned, stirring frequently.

Sprinkle over the flour and stir until well blended. Pour in the white wine and broth and bring to a boil. Skim off any scum that rises to the surface, then reduce the heat and simmer gently for 45 minutes. Stir in the brandy, if using.

Preheat the broiler. Rub each slice of toasted French bread with the cut side of the garlic clove. Place six or eight ovenproof soup bowls on a baking sheet and fill about three-quarters full with the onion soup.

Float a piece of toast in each bowl. Top the toast with grated cheese, dividing it evenly among the soup bowls, and broil about 6 inches from the heat for about 3–4 minutes until the cheese melts and is just beginning to bubble. Serve immediately.

FISH AND GARLIC SOUP

Italian in origin, this soup contains a delightful mix of fish flavored with garlic.

Serves 4

2 tablespoons olive oil

1 onion, thinly sliced

a few saffron strands

1 teaspoon dried thyme

large pinch of cayenne pepper

2 garlic cloves, finely chopped

2 × 14-ounce cans peeled tomatoes,
     drained and chopped

3/4 cup dry white wine

8 cups fish broth

12 ounces skinless whitefish fillets, cut
     into pieces

1 pound monkfish, membrane
     removed, cut into pieces

1 pound mussels in the shell,
     thoroughly scrubbed

8 ounces small squid, cleaned and cut
     in rings

2 tablespoons chopped fresh parsley

salt and ground black pepper

thickly sliced bread, to serve

Heat the oil in a large, heavy-based saucepan. Add the onion, saffron, thyme, cayenne pepper, and salt to taste, stir well, and cook over low heat for 8–10 minutes until softened. Add the garlic; cook for 1 minute.

Stir in the tomatoes, wine, and fish broth. Bring to a boil and boil for 1 minute, then reduce the heat and simmer for 15 minutes.

Add the fish fillet and monkfish pieces to the saucepan and simmer gently for 3 minutes more.

Add the mussels and squid and simmer for about 2 minutes until the mussels open. Stir in the parsley. Season to taste with salt and pepper. Ladle into warmed soup bowls and serve immediately with thickly sliced bread.

GARLIC AND CHILI DIP

Plainly cooked fish can sometimes be rather bland. This garlicky dip will spice it up. Or try the dip with lightly battered, deep-fried vegetables.

Serves 4

1 small red chili
1-inch piece fresh ginger root
2 garlic cloves, peeled
1 teaspoon mustard powder
1 tablespoon chili sauce
2 tablespoons olive oil
2 tablespoons light soy sauce
juice of 2 limes
2 tablespoons chopped fresh parsley
salt and ground black pepper

COOK'S TIP
Large shrimp are ideal served with this sauce. Remove the shells but leave the tails intact so there is something to hold on to for dipping in the sauce.

Halve the chili, remove the seeds, stalk, and membrane, and chop finely. Peel and roughly chop the ginger.

Crush the chili, ginger, garlic, and mustard powder to a paste, using a mortar and pestle.

In a bowl, mix together all the remaining ingredients, except the parsley. Add the paste and blend it in. Cover and chill in the fridge for 24 hours.

Stir in the parsley and season to taste with salt and pepper. Serve in small individual bowls for dipping.

GARLICKY GUACAMOLE

This fresh-tasting spicy dip is made using peas instead of the traditional avocados.

Serves 4–6

3 cups frozen peas, defrosted

2 garlic cloves, crushed

2 scallions, trimmed and chopped

1 teaspoon finely grated rind and juice
   of 1 lime

1/2 teaspoon ground cumin

dash of Tabasco sauce

1 tablespoon mayonnaise

2 tablespoons chopped fresh cilantro

salt and ground black pepper

pinch of paprika and lime slices,
   to garnish

For the crudités

6 baby carrots

2 celery stalks

1 red-skinned apple

1 pear

1 tablespoon lemon or lime juice

6 baby corn

Place the peas, garlic cloves, scallions, lime rind and juice, cumin, Tabasco sauce, mayonnaise, and salt and pepper in a food processor or blender and process for a few minutes until smooth.

Add the chopped cilantro and process for a few more seconds. Spoon into a serving bowl, cover with plastic wrap, and chill in the fridge for 30 minutes, to let the flavors develop.

To make the crudités, trim and peel the carrots. Halve the celery stalks lengthwise and trim into sticks, the same length as the carrots. Quarter, core, and thickly slice the apple and pear, then dip into the lemon or lime juice. Arrange with the baby corn on a platter. Sprinkle the paprika over the guacamole. Serve garnished with lime slices.

BELL PEPPER AND GARLIC SALAD

This salad is enhanced by a garlic and lemon dressing.

Serves 4

2 red bell peppers, halved and seeded

*2 yellow bell peppers, halved
  and seeded*

⅔ cup olive oil

1 onion, thinly sliced

2 garlic cloves, crushed

squeeze of lemon juice

chopped fresh parsley, to garnish

Broil the bell pepper halves for about 5 minutes, until the skin has blistered and blackened. Put them into a plastic bag, seal, and leave for about 5 minutes.

Meanwhile, heat 2 tablespoons of the olive oil in a frying pan. Add the onion and cook over moderately high heat for 5–6 minutes until softened.

Take the bell peppers out of the bag and peel off the skins. Discard the pepper skins and seeds and slice each pepper half into fairly thin strips.

Place the bell peppers, onion, and any oil left in the pan in a bowl. Add the crushed garlic and pour on the remaining olive oil, add a good squeeze of lemon juice and season to taste with salt and pepper. Mix well, cover, and marinate for 2–3 hours, stirring the mixture once or twice.

To serve, garnish the bell pepper salad with the chopped fresh parsley.

Fish and Shellfish

Garlic, in combination with other delicious ingredients

such as saffron, fresh herbs, wine and Parmesan cheese,

lends its delightful pungency to fish sauces, bakes,

tartlets and sautées.

HAKE IN WINE AND GARLIC SAUCE

Cod and haddock cutlets will work just as well as hake in this tasty fish dish.

Serves 4

2 tablespoons olive oil

2 tablespoons butter

1 onion, chopped

3 garlic cloves, crushed

1 tablespoon flour

¹/₂ teaspoon paprika

4 hake steaks, about 6 ounces each

8 ounces fine green beans, cut into

   1-inch lengths

1¹/₂ cups fish broth

²/₃ cup dry white wine

2 tablespoons dry sherry

16–20 live mussels in the shell,

   thoroughly scrubbed

3 tablespoons chopped fresh parsley

salt and ground black pepper

crusty bread, to serve

Heat the oil and butter in a frying pan. Add the onion and cook over moderately high heat for 5 minutes until softened, but not browned. Add the crushed garlic and cook for 1 minute more.

Mix together the flour and paprika, then lightly dust over the hake steaks. Push the onion and garlic to one side of the pan.

Add the hake steaks to the pan and fry until golden on both sides. Stir in the beans, broth, wine, and sherry and season to taste with salt and pepper. Bring to a boil and cook for about 2 minutes.

Add the mussels and parsley, cover the pan, and cook for 5–8 minutes until the mussels have opened.

Serve the hake in warmed soup bowls with plenty of crusty bread.

HALIBUT WITH GARLIC AND TOMATO SAUCE

Sauce vièrge, an uncooked mixture of tomatoes, garlic, aromatic fresh herbs, and olive oil, can either be served at room temperature or, as in this dish, slightly warm.

Serves 2

3 large, ripe beefsteak tomatoes, peeled, seeded, and chopped

2 shallots or 1 small red onion, finely chopped

2 garlic cloves, crushed

6 tablespoons chopped mixed fresh herbs, such as parsley, cilantro, basil, tarragon, chervil, and chives

½ cup extra virgin olive oil

4 halibut fillets or steaks, about 6–7 ounces each

salt and ground black pepper

green salad, to serve

Mix together the tomatoes, shallots or onion, garlic, and herbs in a bowl. Stir in the oil and season to taste with salt and ground black pepper. Cover the bowl and let the sauce stand at room temperature for about 1 hour to allow the flavors to blend.

Preheat the broiler. Line a broiler pan with foil and brush the foil lightly with olive oil. Season the halibut fillets or steaks with salt and pepper, to taste. Place the fillets or steaks on the foil and then brush with a little extra olive oil. Broil for 5–6 minutes until the flesh is cooked. It should be opaque with the top lightly browned.

Pour the sauce into a saucepan, set over low heat, and heat gently for a few minutes. Serve the fish with the garlic and tomato sauce and a green salad.

GARLICKY BAKED FISH

This simple fish bake, with its delicious flavor of garlic, herbs, tomatoes and saffron is said to have originated with the fishermen on the Côte d'Azur.

Serves 4

3 potatoes

2 tablespoons olive oil, plus extra
for drizzling

2 onions, halved and sliced

2 garlic cloves, very finely chopped

1¹/₂ pounds skinless, thick fish fillets,
such as turbot or sea bass

1 bay leaf

1 thyme sprig

3 tomatoes, peeled and thinly sliced

2 tablespoons orange juice

4 tablespoons dry white wine

¹/₂ teaspoon saffron strands, infused in
4 tablespoons boiling water

salt and ground black pepper

Cook the potatoes in boiling salted water for 15 minutes, then drain through a colander. When the potatoes are cool enough to handle, peel off the skins. Using a sharp knife, slice the potatoes thinly.

Heat the olive oil in a large, heavy-based saucepan. Add the onions and cook over moderately high heat for about 10 minutes. Add the finely chopped garlic and continue cooking for a few minutes more until the onions are soft and golden.

Preheat the oven to 375°F. Layer half the potato slices in an 8-cup baking dish. Cover with half the onion mixture, then season to taste with salt and pepper.

Place the fish fillets on top of the vegetables and tuck the herbs in between them. Top with a layer of tomato slices and then the remaining onions and potatoes.

Pour over the orange juice, wine, and saffron liquid, season with salt and pepper and drizzle a little extra olive oil on top. Bake uncovered for about 30 minutes until the potatoes are tender and the fish is cooked through. Serve immediately on warmed plates.

GARLIC SHRIMP TARTLETS

Tartlets made with crisp layers of filo pastry and filled with garlic shrimp make a tempting appetizer.

Serves 4

For the tartlets

4 tablespoons butter, melted

2–3 large sheets filo pastry

For the filling

½ cup butter

2–3 garlic cloves, crushed

1 red chili, seeded and chopped

12 ounces cooked, peeled shrimp

2 tablespoons chopped fresh parsley
* or chopped fresh chives*

salt and ground black pepper

Preheat the oven to 400°F. Brush four individual 3-inch pie pans with melted butter.

Cut the filo pastry into twelve 4-inch squares and brush with the melted butter. Place three squares inside each pan, overlapping them at slight angles and carefully frilling the edges and points while forming a good hollow in each center. Bake for 10–15 minutes until crisp and golden. Cool slightly and remove from the pans.

To make the filling, melt the butter in a large, heavy-based frying pan. Add the garlic, chili, and shrimp and fry quickly over high heat for 1–2 minutes to warm through. Stir in the parsley or chives and season to taste. Spoon the shrimp filling into the tartlets and serve at once.

COOK'S TIP

Use fresh filo pastry, rather than frozen, then wrap and freeze any leftover sheets.

SEAFOOD AND GARLIC SAUTE

Scallops and shrimp are perfectly complemented by the addition of garlic and basil in this delicious and flavorful seafood dish.

Serves 2–4

6 large sea scallops

6–8 uncooked, peeled large shrimp

flour, for dusting

2–3 tablespoons olive oil

2 garlic cloves, finely chopped

1 tablespoon chopped fresh basil

2–3 tablespoons lemon juice

salt and ground black pepper

COOK'S TIP

To make a richer sauce, transfer the cooked scallops and shrimp to a warmed plate. Pour in 4 tablespoons dry white wine and boil to reduce by half. Add 1 tablespoon sweet butter, whisking until it melts and the sauce thickens slightly. Pour over the scallops and shrimp.

Rinse the scallops under cold running water to remove any sand or grit. Pat them dry using paper towels and cut in half crosswise. Season the scallops and shrimp with salt and pepper and dust lightly with flour, shaking off any excess.

Heat the oil in a large frying pan. Add the scallops and shrimp and cook over high heat. Reduce the heat to moderately high and cook for 2 minutes, then turn the scallops and shrimp and add the garlic and basil, shaking the pan to distribute them evenly. Cook for 2 minutes more until golden and just firm to the touch. Sprinkle over the lemon juice and serve immediately.

BROILED GARLIC MUSSELS

Garlic and fresh herbs enliven mussels, which are presented attractively in their shells.

Serves 4

3–3½ pounds live mussels in the shell

½ cup dry white wine

4 tablespoons butter

2 shallots, finely chopped

2 garlic cloves, crushed

6 tablespoons dried white bread crumbs

4 tablespoons chopped mixed fresh
herbs, such as Italian parsley, basil,
and oregano

2 tablespoons grated Parmesan cheese

salt and ground black pepper

fresh basil leaves, to garnish

Scrub the mussels well under cold running water. Remove the beards and discard any mussels that are open. Place the mussels in a large saucepan with the wine. Cover the saucepan and cook over high heat, shaking occasionally, for 5–8 minutes until the mussels have opened.

Strain the mussels and reserve the cooking liquid. Discard any mussels that still remain closed.

Allow the mussels to cool slightly, then remove and discard the top half of each shell, leaving the mussels on the remaining halves.

Melt the butter in a frying pan. Add the shallots and cook over moderately high heat until softened. Add the garlic and cook for 1–2 minutes more.

Stir in the bread crumbs and cook, stirring, until lightly browned. Remove the pan from the heat and stir in the herbs. Moisten with a little of the reserved mussel liquid, then season to taste with salt and pepper.

Spoon the bread crumb mixture over the mussels in their shells and arrange on baking sheets. Sprinkle with the grated Parmesan.

Cook the mussels under a hot broiler in batches for about 2 minutes, until the topping is crisp and golden. Keep the cooked mussels warm in a low oven while broiling the remainder. Garnish with the fresh basil leaves and serve immediately.

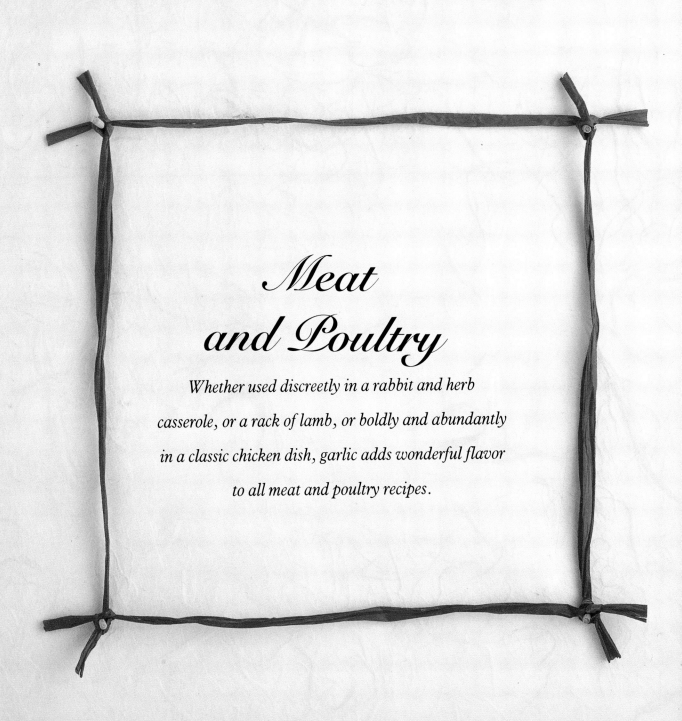

Meat and Poultry

Whether used discreetly in a rabbit and herb

casserole, or a rack of lamb, or boldly and abundantly

in a classic chicken dish, garlic adds wonderful flavor

to all meat and poultry recipes.

GARLIC, PORK, AND PEANUT SATE

These skewers of pork are cooked and served with a delicious garlic and peanut sauce.

Serves 4

1¾ cups long grain rice

1 pound lean pork

pinch of salt

quartered limes, to garnish

For the baste and dip

1 tablespoon vegetable oil

1 small onion, chopped

2 garlic cloves, crushed

½ teaspoon hot chili sauce

1 tablespoon sugar

2 tablespoons soy sauce

2 tablespoons lemon or lime juice

½ teaspoon anchovy essence (optional)

4 tablespoons smooth peanut butter

COOK'S TIP

Indonesian saté can also be prepared using lean beef, chicken, or shrimp.

In a large saucepan, cover the rice with 3¾ cups of boiling salted water, stir, and simmer uncovered for 15 minutes until the liquid has been absorbed. Switch off the heat, cover, and let stand for 5 minutes. Slice the pork into thin strips, then thread zigzag fashion on to sixteen bamboo skewers.

To make the baste and dip, heat the vegetable oil in a saucepan. Add the onion and cook over gentle heat for about 3–4 minutes to soften without coloring. Add the next five ingredients and the anchovy essence, if using. Simmer briefly, then stir in the peanut butter.

Preheat the broiler, spoon some sauce over the pork satés; cook for 8 minutes, turning once. Put the rice on a serving dish, place the pork satés on top, and serve with the sauce. Garnish with the limes.

ROAST LAMB WITH GARLIC AND BEANS

Leg of lamb is the classic Sunday roast. In this recipe, lamb is generously studded with slivers of garlic, which imbue the meat with a delightful flavor.

Serves 4

6–7-pound leg of lamb

3–4 garlic cloves

dash of olive oil

fresh or dried rosemary leaves

1 pound dried navy or fava beans, soaked overnight in cold water

1 bay leaf

2 tablespoons red wine

2/3 cup lamb or beef broth

2 tablespoons butter

salt and ground black pepper

bunch of watercress, to garnish

Preheat the oven to 425°F. Wipe the leg of lamb with damp paper towels and dry the fat covering well. Cut two or three of the garlic cloves into 10–12 slivers, then, with the tip of a knife, cut 10–12 slits into the lamb and insert the garlic slivers into the slits. Rub with oil, season with salt and pepper, and sprinkle with rosemary.

Set the lamb on a rack in a shallow roasting pan and put in the oven. After 15 minutes, reduce the heat to 350°F and continue to roast for 1½–1¾ hours (about 18 minutes per pound) or until a meat thermometer inserted into the thickest part of the meat registers 135–140°F for medium-rare to medium meat or 150°F for well-done.

Meanwhile, rinse the beans and put in a saucepan with enough fresh water to cover generously. Add the remaining garlic and the bay leaf, then bring to a boil. Reduce the heat and simmer for 45 minutes–1 hour, or until tender.

Transfer the meat to a board and stand, loosely covered, for 10–15 minutes. Skim off the fat from the cooking juices, then add the wine and broth to the roasting pan. Boil over moderate heat, stirring and scraping the base of the pan, until slightly reduced. Strain into a warmed gravy boat.

Drain the beans, discard the bay leaf, then toss the beans with the butter until it melts, and season to taste with salt and pepper. Garnish the lamb with watercress and serve with the navy or fava beans and the hot sauce.

RABBIT WITH GARLIC AND THYME

Garlic and thyme add aromatic flavor to this satisfying casserole.

Serves 4

2¹/₂-pound rabbit

3 tablespoons flour

1 tablespoon butter

1 tablespoon olive oil

1 cup red wine

1¹/₂–2 cups chicken broth

1 tablespoon fresh thyme leaves, or

  2 teaspoons dried thyme

1 bay leaf

2 garlic cloves, finely chopped

2–3 teaspoons Dijon mustard

salt and ground black pepper

Cut the rabbit into eight serving pieces: chop the saddle in half and separate each of the back legs into two pieces; leave the front legs whole.

Put the flour in a plastic bag and season with salt and pepper. One at a time, drop the rabbit pieces into the bag and shake to coat them with flour. Tap off the excess, then discard any remaining flour.

Melt the butter and heat the oil in a large, flameproof casserole. Add the rabbit pieces and cook, turning, over moderately high heat until golden.

Add the wine and boil for 1 minute, then add enough of the broth just to cover the meat. Add the herbs and garlic, then simmer gently, covered, for 1 hour, or until the rabbit is very tender.

Stir in the mustard, season, and strain the sauce. Arrange the rabbit pieces on a warmed serving platter with some sauce and serve the rest separately.

CHICKEN WITH GARLIC

Use fresh garlic if you can find it – there's no need to peel the cloves if the skin is not papery.

Serves 8

4½ pounds chicken pieces

1 large onion, halved and sliced

3 large garlic bulbs, about 7 ounces,
*   separated into cloves and peeled*

⅔ cup dry white wine

¾ cup chicken broth

4–5 thyme sprigs, or ½ teaspoon
*   dried thyme*

1 small rosemary sprig, or a pinch of
*   ground rosemary*

1 bay leaf

salt and ground black pepper

Preheat the oven to 375°F. Season the chicken pieces and put skin-side down in a large, flameproof casserole over moderately high heat. Turn frequently until browned. Remove the chicken and pour off the fat.

Add the onion and garlic to the casserole and cook over moderately low heat, stirring frequently, until lightly browned.

Add the wine to the casserole, bring to a boil, and return the chicken to the casserole. Add the broth and herbs and bring back to a boil. Cover and transfer to the oven. Cook for 25 minutes, or until the chicken is tender and the juices run clear when the thickest part of a thigh piece is pierced with a knife.

Remove the chicken pieces from the pan and strain the cooking liquid. Discard the herbs, transfer the solids to a food processor or blender, and purée until smooth. Remove any fat from the cooking liquid and return to the casserole. Stir in the garlic and onion purée, return the chicken to the casserole, and reheat gently for 3–4 minutes before serving.

RACK OF LAMB WITH GARLIC CRUST

This recipe is perfect for entertaining. You can coat the lamb with the garlicky crust before your guests arrive, and put it in the oven when you sit down for the appetizer.

Serves 6–8

3 racks of lamb (about 7–8 ribs each),
trimmed of fat, bones
"French" trimmed
2–3 garlic cloves
4 ounces (about 4 slices) white or
whole wheat bread, torn into pieces
1½ tablespoons fresh thyme leaves or
1 tablespoon rosemary leaves
1½ tablespoons Dijon mustard
ground black pepper
2 tablespoons olive oil
fresh rosemary, to garnish
new potatoes, to serve

Preheat the oven to 425°F. Trim any remaining fat from the lamb, including the fat covering over the meat.

Drop the garlic cloves through the feed tube of a food processor fitted with a metal blade with the machine running. Process until they are very finely chopped then add the whole wheat bread, thyme or rosemary, Dijon mustard, and a little black pepper and process until well combined, then slowly pour in the olive oil.

Press the mixture on to the meaty side and ends of the racks, completely covering the surface.

Put the racks of lamb in a shallow roasting pan, and roast for about 25 minutes for medium-rare or about 3–5 minutes more for medium (a meat thermometer inserted into the thickest part of the meat should register 135–140°F for medium-rare to medium). Transfer the meat to a carving board or warmed platter. With a sharp knife, carefully cut down between the bones to carve into chops. Serve the lamb garnished with fresh rosemary and accompanied by boiled new potatoes.

COOK'S TIP

"French" trimming simply
means scraping off all meat
and skin from the ends of the
rib bones.

Pasta, Pizza, and Grains

Garlic is the perfect foil for mild-tasting grains

and pasta, adding distinctive zest to eggplant lasagne,

asparagus risotto, simple spaghetti, vegetable paella,

pumpkin ravioli and pizza.

WHEAT WITH GARLIC AND FENNEL

This colorful salad combines aniseed, garlic, and citrus flavors.

Serves 4

¾ *cup cracked wheat*

1 large fennel bulb, finely chopped

4 ounces green beans, chopped
and blanched

1 small orange

2 garlic cloves, crushed

2–3 tablespoons sunflower oil

1 tablespoon white wine vinegar

salt and ground black pepper

½ red or orange bell pepper, seeded
and finely chopped, to garnish

Place the wheat in a bowl and cover with boiling water. Leave for 10–15 minutes, stirring occasionally. When doubled in size, drain well and squeeze out any excess water.

While still slightly warm, stir in the chopped fennel and the green beans. Finely grate the orange rind into a bowl. Peel and segment the orange and stir into the wheat salad.

Add the crushed garlic to the grated orange rind in a bowl, then add the sunflower oil and white wine vinegar, season to taste with salt and black pepper, and mix thoroughly. Pour this dressing over the salad, and mix well. Chill the salad in the fridge for 1–2 hours. Serve the salad sprinkled with the finely chopped red or orange bell pepper.

PASTA WITH GARLICKY VEGETABLES

A hearty dish to be eaten with crusty bread and washed down with a robust red wine. Try barbecuing the vegetables and garlic for a really smoky flavor.

Serves 4

1 eggplant

2 zucchini

1 red bell pepper

8 garlic cloves, unpeeled

about 2/3 cup extra virgin olive oil

salt and ground black pepper

1 pound pappardelle

a few fresh thyme sprigs, to garnish

country bread, to serve

Preheat the broiler to moderately high. Wash, then slice the eggplant and zucchini lengthwise.

Halve the bell pepper, cut out the stalk and white pith and scrape out the seeds. Slice the pepper lengthwise into 8 pieces.

Line a broiler pan with foil and arrange the vegetables and unpeeled garlic in a single layer on top. Brush the vegetables and garlic liberally with oil and season well with salt and pepper.

Broil the vegetables until they are slightly charred, turning them once. If they won't all fit in the broiler pan in a single layer, then cook the vegetables in batches.

Cool the garlic, remove the charred skins, and halve. Toss the vegetables with olive oil and keep warm.

Meanwhile, cook the pasta in plenty of boiling salted water according to the instructions on the package. Drain well and toss with the broiled vegetables. Serve immediately, garnished with sprigs of thyme and accompanied by plenty of country bread.

SPAGHETTI OLIO E AGLIO

This is a classic recipe from Rome. A quick and filling dish, it was originally the food of the poor using nothing more than pasta, garlic, and olive oil, but is now fast becoming fashionable.

Serves 4

2 garlic cloves, peeled

2 tablespoons chopped fresh parsley

1/2 cup olive oil

1 pound spaghetti

salt and ground black pepper

Finely chop the garlic and roughly chop the parsley.

Heat the olive oil in a saucepan. Add the garlic and a pinch of salt and cook over low heat, stirring all the time, until golden. If the garlic becomes too brown, it will taste bitter.

Meanwhile, cook the spaghetti in plenty of boiling salted water according to the instructions on the package. Drain well.

Toss with the warm – not sizzling – garlic and oil, and add plenty of black pepper and the parsley. Serve immediately.

PROSCIUTTO AND GARLIC PIZZA

Here is a pizza full of rich and varied flavors. For a delicious variation use mixed cultivated mushrooms.

Serves 2–3

1 bunch scallions

4 tablespoons olive oil

8 ounces mushrooms, sliced

2 garlic cloves, chopped

1 pizza base, about
10–12-inch diameter

8 slices prosciutto

4 bottled artichoke hearts in oil,
drained and sliced

4 tablespoons shredded
Parmesan cheese

salt and ground black pepper

thyme sprigs, to garnish

Preheat the oven to 425°F. Trim the scallions, then chop all the white and some of the green stems.

Heat 2 tablespoons of the olive oil in a frying pan. Add the scallions, mushrooms and garlic and fry over moderate heat until all the juices have evaporated. Season to taste with salt and pepper and let cool.

Put the pizza base on a baking sheet and brush with half of the remaining oil. Arrange the prosciutto, mushrooms, and artichoke hearts on top.

Sprinkle the Parmesan cheese over, then drizzle the remaining oil over and season. Bake the pizza for 15–20 minutes. Garnish with thyme sprigs and serve immediately.

ASPARAGUS AND GARLIC RISOTTO

An authentic Italian risotto has a unique creamy texture achieved by constant stirring of the arborio rice,
available from supermarkets or gourmet stores.

Serves 4

¼ teaspoon saffron strands

about 2½ cups hot vegetable broth

2 tablespoons butter

2 tablespoons olive oil

1 large onion, finely chopped

2 garlic cloves, finely chopped

1¼ cups arborio rice

1¼ cups dry white wine

8 ounces asparagus tips, or asparagus
cut into 2-inch lengths, cooked

¾ cup finely shredded Parmesan cheese

salt and ground black pepper

Parmesan shavings and fresh basil
sprigs, to garnish

ciabatta bread rolls and salad, to serve

Sprinkle the saffron strands over the hot vegetable broth and leave to stand for about 5 minutes to infuse. Meanwhile, heat the butter and olive oil in a large frying pan. Add the finely chopped onion and garlic and fry for about 6 minutes until softened.

Add the rice and stir-fry for 1–2 minutes to coat the grains with the butter and oil. Pour on 1¼ cups of the hot vegetable broth and saffron mixture. Cook gently over moderate heat, stirring frequently, until all the liquid has been absorbed.

Repeat with another 1¼ cups of the broth. When that has been absorbed, add the wine and continue cooking and stirring frequently until the rice has a creamy consistency.

Add the cooked asparagus tips or pieces and the remaining broth and cook, stirring, until all the liquid is absorbed and the rice is tender. Stir in the finely shredded Parmesan cheese and season to taste with salt and black pepper.

Spoon the risotto on to warmed plates and garnish with the Parmesan cheese shavings and fresh basil sprigs. Serve with hot ciabatta rolls and a crisp green salad.

Eggplant and Garlic Lasagne

A great variation on beef lasagne, the eggplants absorb the flavors of tomatoes, herbs and garlic.

Serves 4

3 eggplants, sliced

5 tablespoons olive oil

2 large onions, finely chopped

2 × 14-ounce cans chopped tomatoes

1 teaspoon dried mixed herbs

2–3 garlic cloves, crushed

6 sheets no pre-cook lasagne

salt and ground black pepper

mixed salad, to serve

For the cheese sauce

2 tablespoons butter

2 tablespoons plain flour

1¼ cups milk

½ teaspoon mustard

1 cup shredded sharp Cheddar cheese

1 tablespoon shredded Parmesan cheese

Put the eggplant slices in layers in a colander with salt and leave for 30 minutes over a plate to catch any juices. Rinse and drain.

Heat 4 tablespoons of the oil in a large saucepan. Add the eggplant and fry until brown. Drain on paper towels. Add the remaining oil to the pan, cook the onions for 5 minutes, then stir in the tomatoes, herbs, garlic, and salt and pepper. Bring to a boil and simmer, covered, for 30 minutes.

To make the cheese sauce, melt the butter in a saucepan, stir in the flour and cook over low heat for 1 minute, stirring constantly. Gradually stir in the milk. Bring to a boil, stirring all the time, and cook for 2 minutes. Remove from the heat and stir in the mustard, cheeses, and salt and pepper.

Preheat the oven to 400°F. Place half of the eggplants in an ovenproof dish, spoon over half of the tomato sauce. Place three sheets of lasagne on top. Repeat. Top with cheese sauce, cover and bake for 30 minutes. Uncover after 20 minutes to brown the top. Serve with a mixed salad.

GARLICKY VEGETABLE PAELLA

Bring the paella pan to the table and let people help themselves.

Serves 4

*pinch of saffron strands or 1 teaspoon
  ground turmeric*

3²/₃ cups hot vegetable broth

6 tablespoons olive oil

2 large onions, sliced

3 garlic cloves, chopped

1¼ cups long grain rice

⅓ cup wild rice

*6 ounces pumpkin or butternut
  squash, chopped*

6 ounces carrots, cut into matchsticks

1 yellow bell pepper, seeded and sliced

4 tomatoes, peeled and chopped

4 ounces oyster mushrooms, quartered

salt and ground black pepper

*strips of red, yellow, and green bell
  pepper, to garnish*

Place the saffron in a bowl with 3–4 tablespoons of the boiling broth. Leave for 5 minutes. Heat the oil in a paella pan or large, heavy-based frying pan. Add the onions and garlic and cook over low heat until softened.

Add the rices and toss for 2–3 minutes until coated in oil. Add the broth to the pan with the pumpkin or squash, and the saffron strands and liquid or turmeric. Stir as it comes to a boil and reduce the heat to minimum.

Cover with a pan lid or foil and cook very gently for about 15 minutes. (Avoid stirring unnecessarily as this lets out the steam and moisture.) Add the carrots, bell pepper, tomatoes, and salt and pepper, cover again and leave for 5 minutes more, or until the rice is almost tender.

Add the oyster mushrooms and cook, uncovered, until the mushrooms are just soft. Serve topped with the bell peppers.

GARLIC AND PUMPKIN RAVIOLI

A stunning herb pasta with a superb creamy pumpkin, sun-dried tomato, and roast garlic filling.

Serves 4–6

scant 1 cup flour

2 eggs

pinch of salt

3 tablespoons chopped fresh cilantro

cilantro sprigs, to garnish

For the filling

4 garlic cloves, unpeeled

*1 pound pumpkin, peeled and
    seeds removed*

1/2 cup ricotta cheese

*4 halves sun-dried tomatoes in olive
    oil, drained and finely chopped, with
    2 tablespoons of the oil reserved*

ground black pepper

Place the flour, eggs, salt, and chopped fresh cilantro in a food processor. Pulse until well combined.

Place the dough on a lightly floured board and knead well for 5 minutes, until smooth. Wrap the dough in plastic wrap and leave to rest in the fridge for 20 minutes.

Preheat the oven to 400°F. Place the garlic cloves on a baking sheet and bake for 10 minutes until softened. Steam the pumpkin for 5–8 minutes until tender, then drain well in a colander. Peel the garlic cloves and mash into the pumpkin together with the ricotta and drained sun-dried tomatoes. Season the purée with black pepper.

Divide the pasta into four pieces and flatten slightly. Using a pasta machine, on its thinnest setting, roll out each piece. Leave the sheets of pasta on a clean dish towel until slightly dried.

Using a 3-inch crinkle-edged round cutter, stamp into thirty-six rounds. Top eighteen of the rounds with a teaspoonful of mixture, brush the edges with water and place another round of pasta on top. Press firmly all around the edges to seal. Bring a large saucepan of water to a boil, add the ravioli, and cook for just 3–4 minutes. Drain well and toss with the reserved sun-dried tomato oil. Serve garnished with a few cilantro sprigs.

Vegetable Dishes

*A combination of simple ingredients robustly seasoned
with garlic adds up to fabulous flavor in an exciting
collection of dishes, including pâté, simple mashed
potatoes, galettes, frittata and tamale pie.*

EGGPLANT AND ROAST GARLIC PATE

This simple pâté of eggplant, pink peppercorns, and red bell peppers has more than a hint of garlic!

Serves 4

3 eggplants

2 red bell peppers

5 garlic cloves, unpeeled

1½ teaspoons pink peppercorns in brine, drained and crushed

2 tablespoons chopped fresh cilantro

Preheat the oven to 400°F. Arrange the whole eggplants, peppers, and garlic cloves on a baking sheet and place in the oven. After 10 minutes remove the garlic cloves and turn over the eggplants and bell peppers.

Peel the garlic cloves and place in a food processor or blender. After another 20 minutes remove the blistered and charred bell peppers from the oven and place in a plastic bag. Leave to cool. After another 10 minutes remove the eggplants from the oven. Split in half and scoop the flesh into a strainer placed over a bowl. Press the flesh with a spoon to remove the bitter juices.

Add the eggplant to the garlic in the food processor or blender and blend until smooth. Place in a large mixing bowl. Peel and chop the red bell peppers and stir into the eggplant mixture. To serve, mix in the peppercorns and fresh cilantro.

GARLIC MASHED POTATOES

These creamy potatoes, generously flavored with garlic, are perfect with roasted or sautéed meats.

Serves 6–8

*2 garlic bulbs, separated into
   cloves, unpeeled*

1/2 cup sweet butter

*3 pounds baking potatoes, peeled
   and quartered*

1/2–3/4 cup milk

salt and ground white pepper

Cook the garlic in boiling water for 2 minutes. Drain and peel, then fry over low heat in half of the butter for 25 minutes, stirring occasionally. Do not brown. Spoon into a blender or food processor and process until smooth. Put the purée in a bowl and cover the surface with plastic wrap.

Cover the potatoes in cold water, salt generously, bring to a boil and cook until tender. Drain, and work through a food mill or press through a sifter and return to the pan. Dry over moderate heat, stirring with a wooden spoon, for 2 minutes.

Warm the milk until bubbles form around the edge. Gradually beat into the potatoes with the remaining butter, reserved garlic purée, and salt and white pepper to taste.

COOK'S TIP

This recipe makes a very light, creamy purée. Use less milk to achieve a firmer purée, more for a softer purée. Be sure the milk is almost boiling or it will cool the potato mixture. Keep the potato purée warm in a bowl over simmering water.

BEANS WITH GARLIC AND TOMATOES

This colorful combination of Provençal flavors makes a pleasant change from plain green beans.

Serves 4

1 pound ripe tomatoes

1 tablespoon olive oil

1 shallot, finely chopped

2 garlic cloves, very finely chopped

8 ounces green beans, trimmed and cut into 2–3 pieces

2 tablespoons chopped fresh basil

salt and ground black pepper

Bring a large saucepan of water to a boil. Score a shallow cross in the base of each tomato and plunge them into the boiling water for about 45 seconds, then plunge into cold water. Peel off the skins, halve the tomatoes, and scoop out and discard the seeds. Chop coarsely.

Heat the oil in a large, heavy-based saucepan. Add the shallot and garlic and cook for 2–3 minutes. Add the chopped tomatoes and cook for about 10 minutes until the liquid has evaporated and the tomatoes are soft, stirring frequently. Season to taste with salt and pepper.

Bring a large saucepan of salted water to a boil, then add the beans and cook for 4–6 minutes until just tender. Drain the beans and stir into the tomato mixture with the basil, then cook for 1–2 minutes. Serve immediately or, if you like, let cool for 1–2 hours before serving.

BEAN AND GARLIC TAMALE PIE

A hearty vegetable pie with a substantial polenta topping, sprinkled with cheese.

Serves 4

2 ears of fresh corn

2 tablespoons vegetable oil

1 onion, chopped

2 garlic cloves, crushed

1 red bell pepper, seeded and chopped

2 green chilies, seeded and chopped

2 teaspoons ground cumin

1 pound ripe tomatoes, peeled, seeded,
  and chopped

1 tablespoon tomato paste

14-ounce can red kidney beans, drained

1 tablespoon chopped fresh oregano

salt and ground black pepper

oregano leaves, to garnish

For the topping

1 cup polenta

1 tablespoon flour

2 teaspoons baking powder

1 egg, lightly beaten

½ cup milk

1 tablespoon butter, melted

4 tablespoons shredded Cheddar cheese

Preheat the oven to 425°F. Remove the outer husks and silky threads from the ears of corn, then parboil in boiling, but not salted, water for 8 minutes. Drain and leave until cool enough to handle, then run a sharp knife down the ears of corn to remove the kernels.

Heat the oil in a large saucepan. Add the onion, garlic, and bell pepper and fry for 5 minutes until softened. Add the chilies and cumin and fry for 1 minute more.

Stir in the tomatoes, tomato paste, beans, corn kernels, and oregano. Season. Bring to a boil, then simmer, uncovered, for 10 minutes.

To make the topping, mix together the polenta, flour, ½ teaspoon salt, baking powder, egg, milk, and butter in a large bowl to make a smooth, thick batter.

Transfer the corn kernels and beans to an ovenproof dish, spoon the polenta mixture over the top and spread it out evenly. Bake the tamale pie for 30 minutes. Remove from the oven, sprinkle over the Cheddar cheese, then return to the oven for 5–10 minutes more, until golden and bubbling. Serve immediately.

VEGETABLE AND GARLIC STEW

The combination of vegetables in this stew – a classic in France – is infinitely flexible. Use the recipe as a guide for making the most of what you have on hand.

Serves 4

*1½ pounds ripe tomatoes, or 2 cups
    canned crushed tomatoes*

2 eggplants, about 1 pound total

4–5 tablespoons olive oil

1 large onion, halved and sliced

2–3 garlic cloves, very finely chopped

*1 large red or yellow bell pepper,
    seeded and cut into thin strips*

2 large zucchini, cut into ½-inch slices

1 teaspoon dried herbes de Provence

salt and ground black pepper

COOK'S TIP

*If you prefer peeled bell pepper,
cut it into quarters, broil skin-
side up until blackened, and put
into a plastic bag until cool.
Peel, core, seed, and cut the
bell pepper into strips. Add to
the stew with the tomatoes.*

If using fresh tomatoes, score their bases, plunge into boiling water for 45 seconds, then into cold. Peel, seed, and chop the flesh.

Preheat the broiler. Cut the eggplant into ¾-inch slices, then brush the slices with olive oil on both sides and broil until lightly browned, turning once. Cut the slices into cubes.

Heat 1 tablespoon of the olive oil in a large, heavy-based saucepan or flameproof casserole. Add the sliced onion and cook over moderately low heat for about 10 minutes until lightly golden, stirring frequently. Add the garlic, bell pepper, and zucchini and cook the mixture for 10 minutes more, stirring occasionally.

Add the tomatoes and eggplant cubes, dried herbs, and salt and pepper and simmer gently, covered, over low heat for about 20 minutes, stirring occasionally. Uncover and continue cooking for 20–25 minutes more, stirring occasionally, until all the vegetables are tender and the cooking liquid has thickened slightly. Serve hot or at room temperature.

POTATO AND GARLIC FRITTATA

Fresh herbs make all the difference in this delicious recipe. Try parsley or chives for a change.

Serves 3–4

1 pound small new potatoes

6 eggs

2 tablespoons chopped fresh mint

2 tablespoons olive oil

1 onion, chopped

2 garlic cloves, crushed

2 red bell peppers, seeded and
*   roughly chopped*

salt and ground black pepper

mint sprigs, to garnish

Scrub the potatoes, then cook in a pan of boiling salted water until just tender. Drain, leave to cool slightly, then cut into thick slices.

Whisk together the eggs, mint, and salt and pepper in a bowl, then set aside. Heat the oil in a large frying pan.

Add the onion, garlic, bell peppers, and potatoes to the pan and cook, stirring, for 5 minutes. Pour the egg mixture over the vegetables and stir. Push the mixture into the center of the pan as it cooks to allow the liquid egg to run on to the base. Once the egg mixture is lightly set, place the pan under a hot broiler for 2–3 minutes until golden brown. Serve hot or cold, cut into wedges, and garnished with sprigs of mint.

GARLIC BAKED TOMATOES

If you can find them, use plum tomatoes, which have a warm, sweet flavor. For large numbers of people you could use cherry tomatoes, leave them whole and toss several times during cooking.

Serves 4

3 tablespoons sweet butter

2 garlic cloves, crushed

1 teaspoon finely grated orange rind

4 firm plum tomatoes, or 2 large beefsteak tomatoes

salt and ground black pepper

basil leaves, to garnish

COOK'S TIP

Garlic butter is well worth keeping in the freezer. Make it up as above, or omit the orange rind and add chopped fresh parsley. Freeze in thick slices or chunks ready to use, or roll into a sausage shape and wrap in foil, then cut into slices when partly defrosted.

Soften the butter and blend with the crushed garlic, orange rind, and salt and pepper. Chill for a few minutes in the fridge.

Preheat the oven to 400°F. Halve the tomatoes crosswise and trim the bases so they will sit level. Place the tomatoes in an ovenproof dish and spread the butter equally over each tomato half.

Bake the tomatoes in the oven for 15–25 minutes, depending on the size of the tomato halves, until just tender. Serve, garnished with the basil.

ONION AND GARLIC GALETTES

For a non-vegetarian version, sprinkle some chopped anchovies over the galettes before baking.

Serves 4

4–5 tablespoons olive oil

1¼ pounds red onions, sliced

2 garlic cloves, crushed

2 tablespoons chopped mixed fresh
* herbs, such as thyme, parsley,*
* and basil*

8 ounces ready-made puff pastry

1 tablespoon sun-dried tomato paste

black pepper

thyme sprigs, to garnish

Heat 2 tablespoons of the oil in a frying pan. Add the onions and garlic and cook over low heat for 15–20 minutes, stirring occasionally, until soft but not browned. Stir in the herbs.

Preheat the oven to 425°F. Divide the pastry into four equal pieces and roll out each one to a 6-inch round. Flute the edges and prick all over with a fork. Place the rounds, well spaced out, on baking sheets and chill in the fridge for about 10 minutes.

Mix 1 tablespoon of the remaining olive oil with the sun-dried tomato paste and brush the mixture over the center of each of the pastry rounds, leaving a ½-inch border.

Divide the onion mixture equally between the pastry rounds and spread out. Sprinkle with plenty of black pepper. Drizzle over a little more oil, then bake for about 15 minutes until the pastry is crisp and golden. Serve hot, garnished with thyme sprigs.

GARLICKY BAKED SQUASH

Spaghetti squash is an unusual vegetable – the flesh separates into long strands when baked. One squash makes an excellent supper dish for two. Here it is flavored with garlicky herb butter.

Serves 2

1 spaghetti squash

½ cup butter

3 tablespoons chopped fresh mixed
   herbs, such as parsley, chives,
   and oregano

2 garlic cloves, crushed

1 shallot, chopped

1 teaspoon lemon juice

4 tablespoons shredded
   Parmesan cheese

salt and ground black pepper

Preheat the oven to 350°F. Wash the squash and then cut in half lengthwise. Place the two halves, cut-side down, in a roasting pan. Pour a little water around them, and then bake in the oven for about 40 minutes, or until tender.

Meanwhile, put the butter, herbs, garlic, shallot, and lemon juice in a blender or food processor and process until thoroughly blended and creamy in consistency. Season to taste with salt and pepper.

When the squash is tender, scrape out any seeds and cut a thin slice from the base of each half, so that they will sit level. Place the squash halves on warmed serving plates.

Using a fork, pull out a few of the spaghetti-like strands in the center of each squash half. Add a generous dollop of herb butter, then sprinkle with a little of the shredded Parmesan cheese. Place the remaining herb butter and Parmesan cheese in small serving bowls, and add them to the squash as you pull out more strands.

INDEX

Asparagus and garlic risotto, 44

Bean and garlic tamale pie, 54
Beans with garlic and tomatoes, 53
Bell pepper and garlic salad, 19

Chicken with garlic, 35
Chilis: garlic and chili dip, 17

Dips: garlic and chili dip, 17
   garlicky guacamole, 18

Eggplants: eggplant and garlic
   lasagne, 46
   eggplant and roast garlic pâté, 51
Eggs: potato and garlic frittata, 58

Fennel, wheat with garlic and fennel, 39
Fish: fish and garlic soup, 16
   garlicky baked fish, 24
   hake in wine and garlic sauce, 21
   halibut with garlic and tomato
     sauce, 22
Frittata, potato and garlic, 58

Garlicky baked squash, 62
Garlicky vegetable paella, 47
Green beans: beans with garlic and
   tomatoes, 53
Guacamole, garlicky, 18

Hake in wine and garlic sauce, 21
Halibut with garlic and tomato
   sauce, 22

Lamb: rack of lamb with garlic crust, 36
   roast lamb with garlic and beans, 32
Lasagne, eggplant and garlic, 46

Monkfish: fish and garlic soup, 16
Mussels: broiled garlic mussels, 28
   fish and garlic soup, 16

Navy beans: roast lamb with garlic
   and beans, 32

Olive oil: spaghetti olio e aglio, 43
Onions: onion and garlic galettes, 60
   onion and garlic soup, 14

Paella, garlicky vegetable, 47
Pasta: eggplant and garlic lasagne, 46
   garlic and pumpkin ravioli, 48
   pasta with garlicky vegetables, 40
   spaghetti olio e aglio, 42
Pâté, eggplant and roast garlic, 51
Peanuts: garlic, pork, and peanut
   saté, 31
Peas: garlicky guacamole, 18
Pizza: prosciutto and garlic, 43
Pork: garlic, pork, and peanut saté, 31
Potatoes: garlic mashed potatoes, 52
   potato and garlic frittata, 58
Prosciutto and garlic pizza, 43
Pumpkin: garlic and pumpkin
   ravioli, 48

Rabbit with garlic and thyme, 34
Ravioli, garlic and pumpkin, 48

Red kidney beans: bean and garlic
   tamale pie, 54
Rice: asparagus and garlic risotto, 44
   garlic, pork, and peanut saté, 31
   garlicky vegetable paella, 47

Salad, bell pepper and garlic, 19
Seafood and garlic sauté, 27
Shrimp tartlets, garlic, 26
Soups: chilled tomato and garlic, 13
   fish and garlic, 16
   onion and garlic, 14
Spaghetti olio e aglio, 42
Squash, garlicky baked, 62

Tamale pie, bean and garlic, 54
Tartlets, garlic shrimp, 26
Tomatoes: beans with garlic and
   tomatoes, 53
   chilled tomato and garlic soup, 13
   garlic baked tomatoes, 59
   halibut with garlic and tomato
     sauce, 22

Vegetables: garlicky vegetable paella, 47
   pasta with garlicky vegetables, 40
   vegetable and garlic stew, 56

Wheat with garlic and fennel, 39